FINER GROUNDS

Assured:

Finding Stability in God's Unfailing Promises

A Study of Colossians and Philemon

Kristy Huntsman

To my beautiful daughter Taylor, who put on Christ in baptism just a few months ago. I am so proud of the amazing young lady you have become. I continually pray that you find the stability promised by rooting your life in Christ.

Finer Grounds | Assured: Finding Stability in God's Unfailing Promises

Copyright © 2024 by Kaio Publications, Inc. All Rights Reserved.

All rights reserved. No portion of this book may be reproduced in any form for commercial purposes without the written permission of the Publisher.

Published by Kaio Publications, Inc.
P.O. Box 118
Spring Hill, TN 37174

ISBN: 978-1-952955-48-8

Unless noted otherwise Scripture is taken from NASB is taken from the New American Standard Bible, copyright © 1960, 1962, 1963, 1968, 1971, 1972, 1973, 1975, 1977, 1995 by The Lockman Foundation. Used by permission.

Book edited by Tonya McRady

Design and layout: Kristin Arbuckle (kalt14@gmail.com)

Printed in the United States of America.

Contents

	About Kristy	6
	What Is Finer Grounds?	7
Chapter 1	A Portrait of Paul	9
Chapter 2	Introduction to Colossians	17
Chapter 3	Walk Worthily	25
Chapter 4	Christ's Supremacy	37
Chapter 5	Preparing for Battle	45
Chapter 6	Alive in Christ	53
Chapter 7	Set Your Mind on Things Above	63
Chapter 8	Clothed in Love	71
Chapter 9	Let Christ Rule in Your Heart	79
Chapter 10	Our Godly Influence	87
Chapter 11	Closing Thoughts	95
Chapter 12	Introduction to Philemon	101
Chapter 13	Love on Display	107
	Works Cited	119

About Kristy

Kristy Huntsman is the Editor-in-Chief for ComeFillYourCup.com, a website for Christian women. She has earned her Master's Degree in Biblical Studies from the Bear Valley Bible Institute and a Bachelor's and Master's Degree in music from the University of North Texas and Youngstown State University, respectively. She continues her education through the Greek and Hebrew fluency programs offered by the Biblical Mastery Academy. Kristy and her husband Lance live in Happyland, Oklahoma, with their two daughters, Taylor and Makayla, whom she homeschools. They attend the Stonewall church of Christ, where Lance is the pulpit minister.

What is Finer Grounds?

Finer Grounds is a verse by verse, chapter by chapter, meaty, deep digging study of God's Word. Enrich your personal Bible time or study with a group of ladies. Thought-provoking questions help you reach new levels of faith. Studies are thoroughly researched and passages are expertly explained. Lessons are structured in 13-week (one quarter) segments so you can easily share them with your ladies' Bible class.

Assured: Finding Stability in God's Unfailing Promises
(A Study of Colossians and Philemon)

In today's world, we often find ourselves bombarded by conflicting ideas from people all around us. It often feels like there is nothing that we can be truly assured of in this life. The church in Colossae was dealing with this very issue. They were being pulled in every direction by those who deemed their faith insufficient or just plain ridiculous. In the midst of this chaos, the apostle Paul's letter to the Colossians served as a beacon of hope and stability. Through his words, he reminded them of the foundational truth of their faith in Christ. Paul emphasized the supremacy and sufficiency of Christ, urging the Colossian believers to remain steadfast in their devotion to Christ. He provided them with practical guidance on how to live out their faith in a world full of distractions and false teachings. Paul's message to the Colossians continues to resonate today, offering timeless wisdom and encouragement to believers facing similar challenges in their Christian walk.

Notes

Chapter 1
A Portrait of Paul

I am so thankful that you have chosen to embark on this study with me through the fantastic books of Colossians and Philemon. Throughout this study, we will bask in all the riches and blessings that life in Christ offers as Paul teaches against the destructive heresies entering the church at Colossae. We will also test the boundaries of brotherly love by examining the relationship between an escaped slave and his master, who are now brothers in Christ.

Before we look at these fantastic letters, we should look closer at the man who penned them. Many of you could already fill a book with your knowledge of Paul, but I challenge you to make this more than a piece of academic expertise. As you read about Paul today, imagine how these events mold the man he would become. Think about how these things would influence his ministry in a significant way.

Assured: Finding Stability in God's Unfailing Promise

> Read Philippians 3:5-6. What do these Scriptures tell us about Saul's (Paul's) upbringing?

These verses contain much of what we know about Saul's childhood and younger days. Because of how Jesus spoke to them, we tend to view *Pharisee* as a negative term. While the group as a whole had some major heart problems, we must remember that a Pharisee was simply an expert in the law. It was pride in this position and lack of true love for God that caused Jesus to condemn the Pharisees. F.B. Meyers said, "The word *Pharisee* is a synonym for religious pride and hypocrisy; but we must never forget that in those old Jewish days the Pharisee represented some of the noblest traditions of the Hebrew people. Amid prevailing indifference, the Pharisees stood for a strict religious life.…. Amid the lax morals of the time, which infected Jerusalem almost as much as Rome, the Pharisee was austere in his ideals, and holy in life."

> How would the experience of living the life of a Pharisee have benefited Saul in his future ministry?

Chapter 1 A Portrait of Paul   11

> Read Acts 22:3. What do we learn about Saul's training in this verse?

For a young boy from Tarsus, it would have been an immense honor to journey to Jerusalem to learn. It would have been an even more significant accomplishment to study under Gamaliel, who, in Jewish tradition, is still held as one of the greatest rabbis of all time.

> Read Acts 5:27-42 and summarize the events.

> What can we deduce about Gamaliel based on his response?

This answer could have come from Solomon himself. It is very self-controlled and full of wisdom. Undoubtedly, some of these qualities would have worked their way into the personality of young Saul. Like Moses learning to read and write in the Pharaoh's palace,

God is giving Saul the perfect background and training for the calling he is about to receive.

> God has a habit of using our imperfect pasts as a training ground for our service to Him. What are some ways God has done this in your life?

> Read Acts 8:1. How does Saul participate in the stoning of Stephen?

This is the first mention of Saul's name in Scripture, and it is not good. At first glance, it may appear that he is an innocent bystander; however, upon closer examination, we see that he is in "hearty agreement." The Greek word used is *suneudokeo*, which means to take pleasure with others. It is often used in the context of marriage. Saul isn't simply watching; he is delighting in one of the most tragic events in early church history.

Chapter 1 A Portrait of Paul

> Read Acts 9:1-3. What is Paul doing to the early church?

> Now look at 1 Timothy 1:15-17. How do you think the events of his life before he knew Christ shapes Paul's message?

What a powerful testimony for his ministry! What an extreme 180-degree turn! Indeed, this would have been a reason for people everywhere to stand up and take note. If God has a use for one of Christ's biggest enemies, He could certainly use anyone willing to accomplish His holy purpose.

> Read Acts 9:1-9, 17-20 (Luke's account of Saul's conversion) and Acts 26:9-18 (Paul's account of his conversion). Describe these events in your own words.

> Now read Acts 9:22. How does this verse describe Saul?

This is one of my favorite tidbits from our study today. The word used for "increasing in strength," *endunamoo*, is the same word used to describe Samson's strength in the book of Hebrews. Think of Samson's enormous physical strength and now equate that to the level of Paul's spiritual strength; what an inspiring thought!

Not much is said about Saul's name change to Paul. Luke mentions only briefly in Acts 13:9: "Saul, who was also known as Paul…." From this point on, he is referred to as Paul. Even though not many words denote this transformation, a name change in Hebrew culture is significant.

We aren't told if God changes Paul's name or if he does this on his own; however, there are a few exciting things to note about this. Saul would have been a Hebrew name, and Paul, a Roman name. This change may have signified his transformation from a Hebrew Pharisee to a Gentile minister.

Another interesting point is that he is named after Saul, the first king of Israel. This name would have been prestigious and something unique. The name *Paul* means "little or small." This name change could have signified his position and attitude change from a great teacher and a prominent member of society to "the chief of sinners." It may indicate the humbling process that took place.

While these probably played a part in the name change, I lean toward a third option. When a Biblical name changes, it often indicates that God is taking ownership of a person. We have many examples: Abram to Abraham, Jacob to Israel, and Simon to Peter. These were all men on whom God was putting His stamp. They would no longer be traveling the path they once did; they would now be traveling God's path and working to accomplish His goals. This would now be true of Paul; he would be Christ's companion as he worked to win souls for the Lord!

This week, read through Colossians and Philemon. Remember that these letters were not initially divided into chapters, so read them in one sitting. As you read, try to hear Paul's voice and recognize how his experiences shape his message.

Notes

Notes

Chapter 2
Introduction to Colossians

We spent the past week examining Paul's early life. Now, we find him in prison for preaching the Gospel. Colossians and Philemon are most likely written during Paul's Roman imprisonment.

> Read Acts 28:16, 30-31 and describe Paul's imprisonment in Rome.

Because Paul is a Roman citizen, he is allowed certain freedoms. Even under "house arrest," he continues to preach and teach others. Paul does not waste an opportunity; many of his letters are written from prison. He loves his brothers and sisters in Christ so much that he doesn't want to waste one minute of the time God gives him on this earth.

> Paul doesn't use his bleak circumstances as an excuse to focus on himself. What excuses do you let get in your way when doing God's work? How can you get past some of those this week?

Paul likely heard of the church in Colossae from a slave he encounters named Onesimus (we will learn much more about his story when we arrive at Paul's letter to Philemon). There is no evidence suggesting that Paul has visited the church at Colossae. The work is planted by Epaphras (Colossians 1:7). It is through Epaphras that Paul receives reports about the Colossians (Colossians 1:8).

Colossae was once one of the greatest cities in the Lycos Valley, but after the Roman conquest, it became no more than a "small town." At the beginning of the second century B.C., Antiochus the Great imported around two thousand Jewish families (Martin 17-29). While it is pretty evident that the primary audience of Colossians is Gentile, this would have indicated that there are probably at least some Jewish converts in Colossae. Colossae isn't the only congregation included in this letter, however.

> Read Colossians 4:13. What other cities are included in the initial circulation of this letter?

> Read Revelation 3:14-22 and describe what we learn about the church in Laodicea.

Colossae, Hierapolis, and Laodicea are considered sister cities along the Lycos River. Because of their close proximity, it is reasonable to assume that each city's culture would be similar. In Revelation, we can see that one of the big problems plaguing the area is complacency. The church in Laodicea is accused of being "lukewarm."

Colossae was located on a major east-west trade route, which would have meant it was infused with cultural influences from many different areas. Paul alludes to the fact that many Colossians are converted from paganism. They would have been deeply entrenched in a world of idol worship and false religion. They are in danger of allowing the culture around them to dull their faith, which causes them to compromise in areas they shouldn't. Paul wants them to see what true faith looks like so they could have full assurance of their salvation.

> How have you allowed the culture around you to dull your faith?

> What are some precautions you can take to prevent this from happening?

Despite their challenges, Epaphras brings back a glowing report on the Colossae church. Read the following verses and describe the positive attributes of this church.

- Colossians 1:2

- Colossians 1:4

- Colossians 1:6

This congregation of believers is growing and bearing fruit. Although they are embedded in an ungodly and immoral society, they are a shining light to those around them. What a fantastic testament to the power of the Gospel!

> What challenges does Christ's church face in your community today that hinder its growth? What can you do personally to help overcome these?

This letter is full of encouragement; however, Paul does take some time to warn against threats that will devour the congregation if they are not careful. He warns of false teachers and tries to impart the importance of knowing their obligations to their families. All these issues are addressed within the central theme of the deity and sufficiency of Christ.

> The main theme of Colossians is summed up in Colossians 1:16-18. Rewrite these verses in your own words.

Paul uses several keywords throughout this letter. Not all of these are repeated an extensive number of times, but all are significant to the major themes of the letter. Take some time to read through and mark each time these words (or their synonyms) are used. Try to read through the letter once with each word in mind. This will help you see the various themes and how they fit into the book.

Keywords:
- Wisdom (*sophia*): wisdom that God imparts to those who are close to Him
- Knowledge (*epignosis*): knowledge or recognition, usually referring to God or Christ
- Faith (*pistis*): state of believing based on the reliability of the one trusted; confidence
- Mystery (*mysterion*): not necessarily something unknowable but something hidden from those uninitiated
- Full assurance (*plerophoria/plerophoreo*): convince fully, to be absolutely sure (Arndt, Danker and Bauer)

Also, pay special attention to the use of "all" and "in Him" (or before Him, through Him, etc.)

What do we learn about each of these keywords from Colossians?

Wisdom:

Knowledge:

Faith:

Mystery:

All:

In Him:

Using as many keywords as possible, write a sentence or two describing the theme of Colossians.

Each time you read through this letter, be sure to keep the theme in mind. Remember, these people were facing real problems like you and me. Also, as you continue studying the Colossians book, draw as many parallels as possible between yourself and Paul's audience. The more you understand your similarities, the more this book will come alive with practical teachings you can apply to your everyday life.

Notes

Chapter 3
Walk Worthily

In this chapter, we will begin our verse-by-verse study of the text of Colossians. While it is exciting to dig into the details, we must never forget that this is written as a letter and is meant to be digested as such. I will begin each lesson by asking you to read the letter in one sitting; this shouldn't be too difficult since it is only four chapters long. Doing this each week will give you a fuller understanding of how the individual thoughts fit into the main ideas of the letter.

> Read the entire letter to the Colossians.

We often skim the first few introductory verses as we read the New Testament letters, missing the treasures in these sections. In these opening thoughts, the writers frequently give us the first hints as to the greater purpose of their writing. This week we will focus our entire lesson on Paul's introductory thoughts to the Colossians, particularly his prayer for this congregation.

> **Read Colossians 1:1-2**

Paul begins this letter in his typical fashion: He identifies himself as an apostle and establishes his authority. He also combines the Greek greeting of "grace" with the Jewish greeting of "peace." This would have indicated that this congregation was a mixture of Greeks and Jews.

> How does Paul describe the audience of this letter in Colossians 1:2?

The word *saints* (*hagioi*) that Paul uses here means "holy ones" or "ones set apart for a special purpose." As the church, we are set apart for God's purpose. Today is no different; our congregations of "saints" are still set apart for His purpose. Do we act like a single-minded body working together for a common goal, or do our congregations function more like a social club that meets on Sundays and Wednesdays?

> What can you do this week to change the attitude and mood of your local congregation? How can you start striving to act as if you have been set apart for God's purpose?

Chapter 3 Walk Worthily

Read Colossians 1:3-8

Paul is in constant prayer for his brothers and sisters in Christ. If you pay attention to all the things and people he prays for, it is difficult to see how he has time to do anything else. He understands the power of prayer, and not only that, but he also knows what it means to pray for the things that are in God's will. He also encourages others to "pray without ceasing" (1 Thessalonians 5:17).

Read these verses and describe the circumstances of Paul's prayers.
- Acts 9:1-11

- Acts 14:23

- Acts 21:5

- Acts 28:8

- Romans 1:9-10

This is just a tiny glimpse into Paul's prayer life. There are so many prayers that we could spend an entire quarter on this one aspect of his life. Most of the time, the prayer sections of Paul's letters contain clues to the issues he will address throughout the book. At the beginning of his letter to the church at Colossae, he tells them about his prayer of thanksgiving for them. Imagine what an encouragement it would be to know that Paul was saying a prayer for you!

> Do you thank God for the faithful Christians He has put in your life? List some of the people who have had the biggest impact on your spiritual walk, and be sure to spend time in thankful prayer for them this week. Be sure to let them know that you prayed for them!

> According to Colossians 1:4, what are the two things Paul is so thankful for concerning the church in Colossae?

Epaphras has informed Paul of the Colossians' faith in Jesus and their great love for their brothers and sisters in Christ. This *agape* love that Paul mentions here is not simply a warm fuzzy feeling for someone. *Agape* is a genuine and active love.

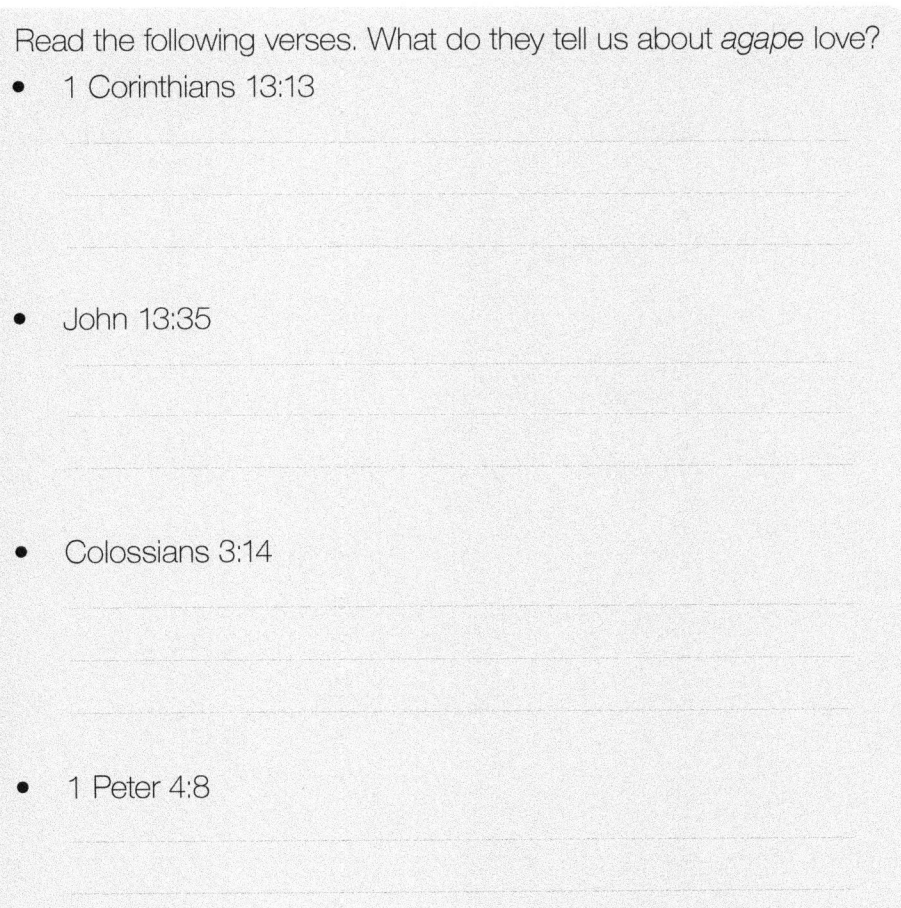

Read the following verses. What do they tell us about *agape* love?
- 1 Corinthians 13:13

- John 13:35

- Colossians 3:14

- 1 Peter 4:8

This congregation is not sitting idly on the sidelines; from the day Epaphras brought them the Gospel message, they have been working diligently for the Lord. There is no stagnant Christianity here. They are consistently growing in number and bearing fruit.

Notice the number of times Paul reminds them that they have already heard the message and know what they need to know. In a world where the surrounding culture is causing their confidence to wane, Paul is trying to bolster their confidence in the truth already written on their hearts.

> **Read Colossians 1:9-12**

Even as well as this congregation was doing, Paul still petitions God for more significant growth.

> According to these verses, what specific things does Paul ask God to grant to the Colossian church?

Paul's prayers are filled with a godly perspective. He isn't asking for people to have material success or even good health; Paul is constantly concerned with the salvation of others. He asks God to grant them qualities that would help them reach Heaven and bring others with them.

Take another look at your prayer life. Do you spend as much time petitioning God to grant you and others spiritual success as you do asking for physical health and material prosperity?

Chapter 3 Walk Worthily

> List some spiritually minded prayer requests for yourself and others that you can focus on this week.

There are four participles Paul lists that describe what it means for them to "walk in a manner worthy of the Lord" (Colossians 1:10-12): bearing fruit in every good work, increasing in the knowledge of God, strengthened with all power, and giving thanks to the Father.

The first of these descriptions, "bearing fruit in every good work," describes people continuously demonstrating their faith through their actions. It is a common theme throughout Scripture that true faith will produce fruit. Jesus even tells His apostles that His faithful followers would be those who bore fruit (John 15:5).

> How can you increase the amount of fruit you bear for the kingdom of God?

The following description given to those who walk worthily is that they are "increasing in the knowledge of God." Many Scriptures are devoted to the importance of knowledge. In verse 9, Paul prays for their knowledge to increase. Knowledge of God's will should be the foundation of our faith.

> Read Romans 10:1-3. What does Paul say about zeal and knowledge?

Zeal alone cannot show us God's will. We must search the Scriptures daily to understand what God expects of us. However, knowledge acquisition should never be simply an academic exercise. As you read through the Scriptures, the knowledge you acquire is only helpful if you put it into practice. You should apply what you learn to your daily walk with God.

> What are some ways you can continually grow in the knowledge of God and put that knowledge into practice?

Chapter 3 Walk Worthily 33

The following participle phrase describes our worthy walk: "strengthened with all power, according to His glorious might." This is a passive participle, meaning we are not the ones doing the strengthening; it is being done to us. Paul includes this in the list to show them that God offers strength and stability to those who are His. This is an incredibly reassuring thought!

> According to Colossians 1:11, what are the two things we attain through this strengthening?

In this passage, we can see that this strengthening leads to steadfastness and patience. *Steadfastness* (*hypomonen*) means the capacity to hold out or bear up in the face of difficulty, and *patience* (*makrothymia*) implies the state of remaining tranquil while awaiting an outcome.

> How do steadfastness and patience improve our Christian walk and make living in this world easier where we are being pressed to compromise our convictions?

Paul's final participle phrase to describe those who walk worthy is "giving thanks to the Father." One who walks worthy continually gives thanks to God. Being able to see how God is good no matter our circumstances is an attribute that will make our Christian walk much easier and more pleasant.

> According to Colossians 1:12, what has God done that they should give thanks for?

The word *qualified* (*hikanoo*) in verse 12 means made sufficient or given everything we need. The idea is that because we are His, God has given us everything we need. This is an incredible confidence boost for us. In a world that continually tells us that we are not enough, Paul tells us we are enough, not because of what we have done, but because of who we are. We belong to God, who has qualified us for an amazing inheritance.

> Do you spend much time in thankfulness daily for God and what He has done in your life? How would this habit change your outlook?

> Read Colossians 1:13-14

Paul uses the standard Scriptural contrast of light and dark in this passage. Jesus rescues us from darkness. Colossians 1:14 says, "In Him, we have redemption, the forgiveness of sins." *Redemption* (*ten apolytrosin*) is release from a painful interrogation, torture, or captivity, and *forgiveness* (*aphesin*) is the act of freeing and liberating from something that confines.

I cannot help but think this statement would have had special significance to Paul during his prison term. The confines of sin are worse than any torture or captivity we can endure, and Jesus has already suffered in our place. Because of His sacrifice, we are released from the "domain of darkness."

The world *kingdom* (*basileia*) refers to the rule and reign of something. When we are transferred out of the "domain of darkness" into the kingdom of Christ, we are trading allegiances. We are no longer allowing the fleshly lusts of the world to rule our decision-making process. Christ should be at the hub of every choice we make.

> How do your decisions demonstrate that Jesus is reigning over your life? How can you improve in this area?

As you go through your week, remember that because of Jesus, you now have access to that glorious light! Pay special attention to your prayers this week. Make sure that they are filled with thanksgiving for Jesus' sacrifice and the commitment of others; also, be sure to ask for spiritual strength for you and your brothers and sisters in Christ.

Notes

Chapter 4
Christ's Supremacy

After last week, it is hard to doubt Paul's love and commitment to the congregation at Colossae. Now, he will give us a glimpse into why he harbors this extreme love and thankfulness. His reason can be summed up in one word: Jesus. Paul devotes a significant amount of ink to describe Christ's unique attributes. Before we begin, be sure that you read the entire letter to keep these verses in context.

Read Colossians 1:15-20

List everything Paul tells us about Jesus in these verses.

Polytheism (the worship of multiple gods) was popular in the pagan society where the Colossians lived. Even if they had converted to Christianity, it would have been easy for them to maintain this mindset. Paul wants to dispel that once and for all. He spends several verses simply discussing the sovereignty and power of Christ.

Not only did Jesus create and rule over all the earth and the heavens, but Paul mentions Jesus several times as the "firstborn." This term would have meant special status, priority, and sovereignty in the day's culture. While listing all these amazing things about Jesus, Paul mentions that He is the head of the church. Paul establishes Jesus' unequivocal authority in all things, specifically their congregation.

Do we behave as though Christ is the supreme authority in our lives? Do you pay more attention to what your preacher or teachers say than what God's Word tells us? Do you study so that you can be sure that you are following the ultimate authority? Are you quick to forget the sovereignty of Christ when it comes to your decision-making? Would He approve of the choices you make on a day-to-day basis?

> How can you remind yourself daily of the sovereignty of Christ?

Chapter 4 Christ's Supremacy

Read Colossians 1:21-23

How does Paul describe their former lives in Colossians 1:21?

The words Paul uses here are interesting. *Alienated* (*apallotrioo*) means excluded or estranged, and *hostile* (*echthros*) is an enemy or one who hates. He uses powerful language to describe their former state of mind. This mindset led to them committing evil deeds.

However, Paul quickly follows up this statement with good news: they have now been reconciled. The act of reconciliation is the breaking down of a barrier. Our sins before Christ were barriers to our relationship with God. We could only approach His throne with them broken down.

How does Paul describe them after Christ reconciles them?

> According to Colossians 1:23, to what condition must we adhere to be presented to God in this way?

Think about the honor it is for us for Christ Himself to present us to God. All our sins and iniquities are a thing of the past. This isn't automatic; we must continue in the faith. In Greek, the words Paul uses here—"established" and "steadfast"—describe a house with a sturdy foundation fixed solidly in its place.

Read Colossians 1:24-29

As we read through Acts and the letters that Paul pens, we get an image of a man who is not afraid to suffer for the cause of Christ. He endures torture, imprisonment, and ultimately death because of his unyielding faith and commitment. At some points, his suffering is so great that he laments life itself (2 Corinthians 1:8-9). Even through all these trials, he counts it a joy to suffer for the sake of other Christians.

When I read about Paul's joy in suffering, I think of a mother during childbirth. She is in extreme pain, and yet most mothers will agree that this process was well worth it once they experience the exhilaration of holding their newborn child. They can have joy during the process because they know that in the end, their reward will be amazing!

Chapter 4 Christ's Supremacy

In the same way, Paul could see how this would end. He knows that more suffering is in store for him, but the joy of seeing his brothers and sisters in Heaven overpower the momentary pain and hardship he faces when serving others.

Are we willing to serve others to the point of our own suffering? It seems our society has compassionate hearts, but only to the point that it doesn't inconvenience us. If something is going to make us push back our bedtime or rearrange our schedule, then it suddenly becomes one of those things someone else can do.

For me, this verse is incredibly humbling. I think of all the little excuses I often come up with for not serving to my total capacity: I am tired, I'd have to find something to do with my daughters, I already have so much to do this week, I need "me" time, etc. I wonder what Paul, who daily suffered things I can't imagine, would think of my frivolous reasoning.

> What are some of the silly excuses you make for not serving others? What can you do this week that you normally find an excuse for?

> How does Paul describe the "mystery" in Colossians 1:26-27?

The mystery that the Jews never fully understood until now is that the Gentiles would also have access to salvation. Paul wants to be sure once again that they understand what a privilege a life in Christ truly is. Because of Christ's sacrifice, every man has access to the throne of God through the Gospel.

> How can reminding ourselves about this mystery reinforce our faith and encourage us to continue steadfastly in our daily walk?

> According to Colossians 1:28, how do we proclaim Jesus?

The two participles describing the verb *proclaim* are admonishing and teaching. We must admonish and teach others so that we can win souls! *Admonishing* is correcting others when they make mistakes, and teaching shows them how to behave correctly. Paul tells us that this is how we can work to bring everyone to Christ.

Admonishing and teaching absolute principles are not popular in our society. We shy away from saying anything that might offend someone else. Remember the suffering that Paul faced for doing this. You may be saving someone's soul by teaching and admonishing in love. It's unpopular and will cause you strife in this life, but try to think about your actions from a heavenly perspective.

> Why are admonishing and teaching important to our Christian walk, and why are they so difficult?

> How can we keep our hearts in check when we need to admonish or teach? How can we show our love for others in these situations?

As you go about your daily routine this week, remember that being a faithful Christian will require you to step outside your comfort zone. Think of ways that you can serve others and teach them the truth, even if it is unpopular or an inconvenience. Make sure you pray and ask God for a spiritual perspective in your day-to-day life.

Notes

Chapter 5
Preparing for Battle

There is no doubt that Paul places great importance on Christ's sovereignty. Most of the letter up to this point has been devoted to this idea, and in chapter 2, Paul continues the idea, extolling the great riches that are available to those who have true knowledge of Christ.

Begin this week by reading Paul's letter to the church at Colossae in its entirety. Remember that the chapter breaks we see were put in later by others to make it easier to reference specific verses. As we begin Colossians 2, the thought flows directly from the previous chapter.

Read Colossians 2:1-3

Again, remember that this continues Paul's idea from the previous chapter. He is still talking about his physical trials in serving them. He has a genuine desire for every person to be "complete in Christ" (Colossians 1:28). The word for *struggle* Paul uses here (*agon*) means to engage in a fight. This is one of many allusions to a spiritual battle throughout this letter.

> According to Colossians 2:2, what is Paul's desire for the church at Colossae?

I love the imagery Paul uses here. He says they are "knit together in love." This week, our puppy found a ball of yarn and pulled it apart; now, it is a huge mess. Looking at it, I thought of the beautiful, crocheted baby afghan one of my dearest friends made for my daughter. This afghan is one of my most cherished possessions and has kept both of my daughters warm. Whenever I see it, I think of the fantastic Titus 2 woman who gave it to me.

The tangled mass of string stretched across my yard is created with the same material as my beautiful afghan. The difference is their catalyst for change. One is the destructive power of a puppy, and the other is the loving, intentional work of a friend's hands. Something wonderful and precious is created by a simple ball of yarn being knit together.

In Paul's example, individual people in the congregation are the yarn. We can allow our love to knit us together into one of the most

Chapter 5 ⟨Preparing for Battle⟩

beautiful creations on this earth—the church. We must actively seek to show this *agape* love to one another, or we may end up like the tangled mass of string in my front yard.

> Are you allowing your love to knit you together with your brothers and sisters in Christ at your local congregation, or do you keep them at arm's length? What can you do this week to begin building a knit-together relationship with someone in your congregation?

> According to Colossians 2:2, where does the wealth to which Paul refers come from?

The only wealth and riches that are worth anything in this life are the ones that come from knowledge of God's mystery. In the last chapter, we discussed that the mystery is Christ and His plan to offer salvation to everyone. The more you study and learn of God and His will for you, the more confident and assured you can be in your salvation. There is no more incredible blessing on this earth than knowing you will end up in Heaven!

This is no new concept in Scripture; Paul is constantly talking about the spiritual blessings found in Christ.

> Read the following verses and list the blessings found in Christ.
>
> - Romans 6:23
>
> - Romans 8:2
>
> - 1 Corinthians 1:30
>
> - Galatians 3:26
>
> - Galatians 3:28
>
> - Ephesians 1:7

- Philippians 3:9

- Philippians 3:14

- 1 Timothy 1:14

- 2 Timothy 2:10

This is only a tiny portion of the Scriptures devoted to the blessings found in Christ. In our society, getting caught up in worldly benefits is easy, even when focusing on godly things. We drop everything to give aid to the tornado victims who lost all their material possessions, but are we as concerned about the salvation of their souls as we are about their housing situation?

We are often granted unique opportunities to impact others and help them physically. Are we using these as chances to open the door to show them the spiritual blessings found in Christ?

How can we do a better job of making sure we emphasize the spiritual blessings available in Christ to those around us daily?

Read Colossians 2:4-7

According to Colossians 2:4, what is Paul's purpose in reminding them of the blessings found in the knowledge of Christ?

If our knowledge of God and His will for us is complete, nothing should be able to move us from our convictions. People could easily deceive me about a medical diagnosis. They could make up some illness that doesn't exist and imaginary symptoms to accompany it; I would most likely fall for their lie hook, line, and sinker. However, they would not be able to pass the same deception on to my friend, who happens to be a doctor.

What is the difference? Well, my friend is an expert on the subject matter. He knows medical language and is immersed in medical

Chapter 5 Preparing for Battle 51

journals daily, learning about everything in his field. We should be this way when it comes to our spiritual life. We need to ensure that we are the experts in our spiritual walk; we should be able to spot false teaching a mile away.

> What are some of the "persuasive arguments" that threaten the church today?

> How can we do a better job of making sure we both individually and as a church are fully assured and not swayed by these pretty-sounding false teachings?

Paul loves this congregation and doesn't want them deceived by the false teachers in their community. He knows that if they are filling their lives with the knowledge and wisdom of Christ, it will be almost impossible for someone to deceive them.

> Are you an "expert" in the field of Christianity? What can you do to have more confidence in your knowledge of God and His will for you? How will you implement these changes this week?

Again, in Colossians 2:5, Paul uses military language. "Good discipline" (*taxis*) is a military term meaning orderly ranks, and "stability" (*stereoma*) means the steadfastness of an army. Picture in your mind the church as the army of God. We have been equipped with the knowledge of Christ, and because of that, we are standing firm, ready for battle.

> Why do you think Paul uses so many references in his letters to armies and battles?

The church at Colossae has received the message of Christ and is firmly rooted in it. Now, this foundation is being built upon, and it is growing. It is becoming a fortress that Satan could not penetrate.

Are you preparing for battle? Are you an expert in your faith? Are you knitting yourself together with your brothers and sisters in Christ to form an army that cannot be overtaken by sin? Is your foundation strong enough to support a fortress that Satan cannot break down?

As you go about your week, be conscious of the battle you are in. The only way to win is to fully rely on the riches and mercy found in Christ. He is offering us a chance to be a part of the winning army, His army. Will you ignore this call to arms, or will you come to Him armed with the sword of truth, ready for battle?

Notes

Notes

Chapter 6
Alive in Christ

Begin this week by reading Paul's letter to the Colossians in its entirety. Throughout the entire letter, you can see Paul explaining to them the importance and deity of Christ. In chapter 2, he will stay focused on this but make it more tangible to his audience. What does this mean for them? How should they behave now that they have this knowledge?

Read Colossians 2:8-15

What is Paul's warning to them in Colossians 2:8?

So much of Paul's letter has been devoted to the true knowledge found in Jesus Christ. He wants them to understand that false teachers will try to sway them from this message. Again, in this section, Paul uses battle language. He doesn't want them "taken captive." They are in a spiritual war, and if they aren't careful, they will find themselves prisoners.

These philosophies and deceptions that people are bringing into the church had their basis in human tradition. The word *philosophy* used here, *philosophia*, literally means "love of wisdom." At this point in history, Gnosticism was coming to prominence. While there were many different sects of Gnosticism, one of the main beliefs was that each man could gain salvation in his own way through gaining knowledge. In this way, they thought they could become a "god" themselves. They felt that Jesus was enlightened but they could surpass even Him if they learned enough.

By repeatedly emphasizing Christ's deity and acknowledging Him as the source of all true knowledge, Paul directly refutes these Gnostic ideas.

> What are some of the human philosophies that threaten to infiltrate the church?

> How can we, as Christians, work to recognize these man-made ideas and actively protect our congregations from being swept up in them?

> What custom does Paul refer to in Colossians 2:11? What is the significance of this act according to Genesis 17:7-13?

It is interesting that Paul brings up circumcision amid the discussion of the manmade philosophies that are threatening the church. While it might initially seem confusing, it makes complete sense when we understand the church in Colossae's situation. The pagan philosophies are just one end of the spectrum causing the Colossian church to worry about their salvation––at the other end is the Jewish philosophies. On one end, they have their old friends pressuring them to continue to participate in pagan rituals, but on the other, they have the Judaizers that are going from town to town, compelling Christians to adhere to the Old Law, which included the act of circumcision. The heart of the issue is the same: They are being tempted to rely on something other than the sufficiency of Christ.

> Why does Paul compare baptism with circumcision?

Circumcision is a sign of the Jew's commitment to God. It means that they are His people. Unless they are circumcised, they are not part of God's covenant. For these reasons Paul equates baptism with circumcision. We now have a spiritual act of circumcision in the form of baptism. Through baptism, we are able to strip off and die to our old sinful lives. This allows us to be raised with Christ to walk a new life. Now, we have been granted forgiveness for all our sins.

In Colossians 2:13, Paul states that baptism has "made [us] alive together with Him." He then lists five participles that describe what God does when we are baptized into Christ:

- Having forgiven us all our transgressions (2:13)
- Having canceled out the certificate of debt (2:14)
- Having nailed it (the certificate of debt) to the cross (2:14)
- Having disarmed the rulers and authorities (2:15)
- Having triumphed over them (the rulers and authorities) (2:15)

Paul reassures them that when they become part of the body of Christ through baptism, God has fulfilled all of their needs. There is no reason to seek absolution anywhere but in Christ.

Many of us know the feeling of being weighed down by debt. Sometimes, we are drowning in debt so much that it seems there is no way out. Imagine if someone today took everything you owed and stamped "PAID IN FULL" on each and every bill. What an enormous relief that would be!

Our debt that is canceled by Christ is infinitely more staggering than simple monetary forgiveness. According to the Law of Moses, we are all guilty because of our sins; death is the punishment. Jesus took this debt and nailed it to the cross. Because of Christ's sacrifice, we no longer owe our lives. We can partake in the blessings of eternal life!

> Do you spend time each day dwelling on the extreme sacrifice that Jesus made to cancel your debt? How can you try to honor Him in your everyday walk?

I love Paul's language in Colossians 2:15. He continues his military references and states that Jesus has "disarmed the rulers and authorities." Through Jesus' death and resurrection, God defeated all opponents of His plan. God publicly exposed and displayed the weakness of all opposing forces by His victory through Jesus. When we are baptized, we allow Jesus to triumph over the rulers and authorities that previously led our path. Christ is victorious every time He wins a soul from the clutches of Satan!

Assured: Finding Stability in God's Unfailing Promise

> **Read Colossians 2:16-23**

Pay attention to Paul's use of the word *therefore*. When it is written, be sure to look and see what it is referencing. In this case, Paul is referring back to all Christ has done for them at baptism. Because He has canceled out their debt and has triumphed over all of the rulers and authorities, they are not subject to man's traditions. The only law they are subject to is the law of Christ.

> What qualifications does Paul give to their freedom in Christ in Romans 14:13-21 and 1 Corinthians 8:8-13?

They have liberty in Christ but are still called to respect their fellow Christians. Their main goal should always be to win and keep souls.

> What does Paul warn the Colossian church about in Colossians 2:18?

"Defrauding you of your prize" (*katabrabeuo*) literally means to rob a prize and refers to the Greek games. Someone might be disqualified if he has not followed the rules precisely or if she has committed a foul. Paul is warning about false teachers who will come in and steer them from the true path of Christianity. In the end, this would cause them to lose their eternal reward.

> Are you continually mindful of what you are being taught and constantly checking it against the Scriptures to make sure it is accurate? How can you keep others from "defrauding you of your prize?"

Paul lists ways that others were trying to deceive them, which are rooted in the issue he addresses in Colossians 2:19. Again, Paul brings the emphasis back to Christ. By buying into these beliefs, they are denying Christ His rightful place as the head of the church. These false teachers have severed the head from the body!

> Paul compares the church to a body many times in Scripture. Explain this comparison according to 1 Corinthians 12:14-26 and Ephesians 4:15-16.

Paul goes on to explain to the Colossian brethren that no life is found in the world's regulations. We aren't governed by those principles; we are governed by Christ and Christ alone. The precepts of the Old Law are physical and will perish. Paul continues to remind them to think spiritually.

As you go about your week, keep in mind Christ's sacrifice for you. You ran up an enormous debt, and with one swift motion, He stamped "PAID IN FULL" on your bill. You have been given so much; do not allow yourself to be deceived by the world. Keep your mind sharp, and don't allow someone to rob you of your heavenly prize!

Notes

Chapter 7
Set Your Mind on Things Above

Much of this letter has been devoted to everything Christ has done for the Colossians. Paul now shifts focus a little; because of everything done on their behalf, he lays out detailed instructions for how they should behave. Once again, read Paul's entire letter to the Colossian church.

Read Colossians 3:1-4

What does Paul tell the Christians in Colossae to do in Colossians 3:1-2?

> What are the "things that are on the earth" according to Colossians 2:16-23?

In a society drowning in sin, Paul wants to ensure that the church in Colossae maintains its spiritual perspective. Paul understands that living day in and day out in a world constantly bombarding you with sin takes its toll. Notice the active verbs he uses here. He doesn't simply tell them to endure; he tells them to "keep seeking" and "set your mind."

It takes constant refocusing to live a genuinely God-centered life. If we don't continually try to focus on God's plan and the things He desires for us, we can easily get sidetracked. In our society, it is challenging to live with the world all around us and keep a godly mindset.

Sometimes, I feel like I am doing commendable work if I simply exist till the end of the day. If I haven't accidentally burnt the house down or lost the children, I view my day as a success. Paul has a different opinion on this. Paul encourages us to think: What is my mindset during the day? Am I drowning in self-pity, or am I serving my family with the love of Christ? Do I seek to do God's will at every chance I get, or do I take the easy way out? Do I diligently teach my children by words and deeds what it means to be a Christian today, or do I ignore them so I can accomplish what I want?

It is not easy to continually seek God's will for our lives. It takes constant dedication and effort and can be exhausting sometimes. Paul doesn't say it was easy, but he does tell us it is expected. Compared to what God has done for us, this is just a drop of water in the ocean.

> Do you always keep God and His plan at the forefront of your mind? What could you do this week to allow yourself and your household to focus on "the things above?"

In Colossians 3:3, Paul tells us we are "hidden" with Christ in God. This word (krupto) means to hide something precious for safekeeping. What a beautiful thought! When it seems that life may engulf you today, keep this in mind: You are God's precious possession, and He is there to keep you safe and hide you away from the troubles you are experiencing. Paul continues and tells us that our ultimate comfort should come in knowing that when Christ returns and is revealed, we will be with Him in glory!

Read Colossians 3:5-11

Paul moves from his general statements about their mental focus and begins to get specific. He starts with the things that should be removed from their lives and then tells them how to replace them.

> According to Colossians 3:5, what should they be "dead" to?

I want to take some time to look at each of these in detail. The temptations that the Colossian church faced have not faded with time. While some have changed forms, they are still prevalent in our society. These sins can still rip our lives to shreds if we allow them to, so it would be a good idea to spend time examining them in the context of our own lives.

The first is *immorality* (*porneia*). It is the word we get pornography from and means every unlawful sexual act. This includes adultery, sexual intercourse outside of marriage, prostitution, and homosexuality. Did you know, according to the Centers for Disease Control and Prevention, that almost 70% of high school seniors are sexually active? My husband and I have worked with the youth in churches long enough to see that, unfortunately, the statistics in the church are not significantly different.

This is not limited to our unmarried members. A poll conducted by MSNBC reveals that 22% of married people admit to cheating on their spouses. Again, while statistics in the church are probably a little lower, this is still a big problem. We must be teaching our children what God's plan for sex is so that they understand the only correct context and adhere to it!

Next, Paul lists *impurity* (*akatharsia*). This is any filthy substance or a state of moral corruption. Think about the things you encounter daily that would fit this category: movies, books, topics of conversation, and music. This list could go on and on. Keep vigilant in barring the filthy things from your life.

Passion (*pathos*) is next on this list. Simply stated, this is a lustful desire. This is not limited to sexual desire, though it would certainly cover that. Anything you yearn strongly for that is not in the will of God would fall into this category. Think back to Paul's statements about placing our minds on godly things; if we are constantly dwelling on our desire and lust for something, we push God out of His rightful place in the forefront of our minds.

Evil desire (*epithumia*), or a desire for something forbidden, is next. This is similar to pathos. The difference is that pathos could be directed at something that isn't inherently bad; epithumia is a focus on something forbidden. Jesus is very clear in His sermon on the mount (Matthew 5–7) that the mind and heart matter. Dwelling on a sinful act is just as bad as committing it.

The final word in this list is *greed* (*pleonexia*). This is desiring more than one deserves or insatiableness. Paul says that this is nothing more than idolatry. Greed runs rampant in our society. Everyone wants what they don't have and feels entitled to what they don't need. There is no place for this attitude in Christianity. This is the opposite of the humble attitude Christ showed us and expects from us.

> Examine this list one more time. Which of these do you struggle with most? How can you work to strip off this behavior?

> According to Colossians 3:6, what will result from these sinful behaviors?

In Colossians 3:8-9, Paul has a second list of sins that he would like the church at Colossae to put aside. While most of the sins listed in verse 5 are personal, the things he lists in verses 8 and 9 are directly reflected in their relationships.

> According to Colossians 3:8-9, what behaviors and attitudes should they put away?

Here are their definitions:
- Anger (*orge*)—state of strong displeasure
- Wrath (*thymos*)—passionate and intense displeasure
- Malice (*kakia*)—a mean-spirited or vicious attitude or disposition
- Slander (*blasphemia*)—speech that degenerates or defames
- Abusive speech (*aischrologia*)—speech that is generally considered in poor taste, obscene speech, dirty talk
- Lying (*pseudomai*)—to tell a falsehood

Unfortunately, most of these can be found within the walls of our congregations. Women are more susceptible to some of these than our male counterparts. How often have you been involved in a conversation where you said something that might be "degenerative or defaming?" Have you ever had a mean-spirited attitude toward one of your brothers or sisters in Christ?

I have heard women in the church say: "I love them, but I don't have to like them." This statement couldn't be further from the truth. It may not be easy, but we must actively seek to show that agape love we see so much in Scripture. We are commanded to build strong relationships with our brothers and sisters in Christ. Remember that afghan we talked about when we looked at Colossians 2? We must ensure we are "knit together" with our fellow Christians.

> Do you struggle with how you think about and speak about others? What can you do this week to build someone up instead of tearing her down?

Remember to constantly refocus on God and His plan throughout your week. Work to remove the impurities from your life and strive to never let defaming speech escape your lips.

Notes

Chapter 8
Clothed in Love

Last week, we focused on the beginning of Colossians 3. Remember that the focus of this letter has been the supremacy of Christ. Paul devotes the first half of the letter to this idea and now begins to show the church at Colossae in very practical terms what that means for their everyday lives. In the previous lesson, Paul admonishes us to strip off our old selves; this week, he tells us about the qualities that should comprise our new life. As always, begin this week by reading Paul's letter to the church at Colossae in one sitting.

Read Colossians 3:12

How does Paul describe the church in Colossae in this verse?

In verse 12, Paul again points out that they are making these changes in their lives because God has chosen them. They are holy, which literally means to be set apart for a purpose. Not only this, but they are his beloved. He intends to continually remind them of the blessings they are privileged to partake in; he wants them to understand that though these changes are extremely difficult, they are worth making because what they have been given is so much greater.

> How can reminding ourselves that we are chosen and loved help us strip off our old self and put on the new self?

In Colossians 3:8, Paul uses the phrase "put them all aside." In Greek, this gives us the image of someone shedding an article of clothing. This old life he describes in great detail is what we should be taking off and throwing out like a worn-out garment. In contrast, Paul commands us in Colossians 3:12 to "put on" certain things. Again, in the original language, this would have implied the image of someone dressing herself. We have stripped the old, smelly clothes of a sinner and now have the privilege of clothing ourselves with royal garments fit for a queen!

According to Colossians 3:12, what qualities make up these royal robes?

Like we did last week with the lists of negative qualities, I'd like to examine each of these positive qualities in detail.

The first of these qualities is *compassion* (*oiktirmos*), which is the idea of displaying concern for the misfortunes of others. In order to display compassion, we must know what our brothers and sisters in Christ are going through. When we learn about a struggle that a member of our Christian family faces, we should show them that we care by praying fervently on her behalf and trying to find ways to meet her physical needs.

Do not simply pray for her once and forget her; make sure that you keep updated on her situation. Though death in the family or some other major life event may only land someone on the church prayer list for one or two weeks, you can be confident that the repercussions of trials like this are almost never-ending. Be sure to remain there for people and show genuine interest in her struggles even after the world has forgotten.

Assured: Finding Stability in God's Unfailing Promise

> What practical ways can you strive to be compassionate toward others this week?

> What are some ways you can keep the struggles of others at the forefront of your mind?

The second on this list is *kindness* (*chrestotes*); it means showing uprightness in one's relationships with others or being helpful or beneficial. Would those around you consider your friendship "helpful or beneficial"? Do you have a positive influence on those around you? We have all known people who have changed our lives in such positive ways that we cannot imagine where we would be without them. Let us strive to be this person in every one of our friendships.

> Do you positively affect your brothers and sisters in Christ, or are you simply in a stagnant relationship? What can you do in your friendships to help and benefit those around you?

Next is *humility* (*tapeinophrosyne*), the idea of putting others above oneself. Remember, earlier in this letter (Colossians 2:23), Paul warns the church about self-abasement or false humility. The humility he mentions in Colossians 3:12 is not obtained by giving lip service to all of our faults. It is not downplaying the abilities and gifts that God has given us. Genuine humility is always considering the needs of others before your own.

Along those same lines, Paul follows up with *gentleness* (*prauteta*). This is the quality of not being overly impressed with one's self-importance. In our society, these qualities are almost non-existent. Every aspect of our lives seems to be "me-driven." This idea that my wants and needs supersede everything and everyone else has had many adverse effects on our culture: a skyrocketing divorce rate, an ever-increasing number of abortions, a lack of commitment, and corrupt business practices, to name a few.

> How has self-centered behavior affected your life? In what ways can you make a conscious effort to put other's needs ahead of your own this week?

The final quality Paul lists in Colossians 3:12 is *patience* (*makrothymia*). This carries the idea of remaining tranquil while waiting for an outcome or while being provoked. We can experience this tranquility by continually keeping our lives in perspective. None of our trials and struggles on this earth are permanent. The only thing that lasts is our eternal reward. It is much easier to continue when we can see a favorable end to our situation; that is exactly what a life in Christ offers us.

Read Colossians 3:13-14

In Colossians 3:12, Paul lists qualities that we should clothe ourselves in. Now, he goes into further detail with specific actions in verse 13 and sums them up in verse 14.

Chapter 8 Clothed in Love   77

What does Paul tell them to do to their brothers and sisters in Christ in Colossians 3:13?

Paul understands that dealing with people would not always be easy. He knows the qualities he lists would take work and constant focus. They would make mistakes and need forgiveness. Remember this when dealing with others. Christ has offered us unlimited forgiveness; to be deserving of this, we must offer this same forgiveness freely to others.

According to Colossians 3:14, what is the ultimate bond that unites Christians?

Agape love is the supreme quality that should rule our relationships. If we have genuine, fervent love for one another, the qualities that Paul lists will be much easier to obtain; in the absence of love, they will be nearly impossible.

The word Paul uses for bond in this section is *syndesmos*; in its most literal form, it means ligament. Paul regularly describes the church as the body of Christ. I do not believe his use of this specific word here is an accident. Without ligaments, the separate pieces of our body would fall apart. The ligaments keep us functioning and moving together as a whole unit.

It is the same with the love we show our brothers and sisters in Christ. If there is no love, our congregation cannot function the way it is intended. There is no way for the body of Christ to work toward a unified and singular goal in its absence. If we don't have love, we will fall to pieces like a skeleton devoid of all ligaments.

As you go about your daily life this week, keep your brothers and sisters in Christ at the forefront of your mind. Be sure to pray for them and find ways to meet their physical needs. Continue showing concern for them after their time on the church prayer list has expired—the only way to be effective as a congregation is to knit yourselves together with one another continually. Attach the ligaments of the Lord's church by showing love to one another. If we accomplish this, our fellowship will be so irresistible to others that they want to partake in it!

Notes

Chapter 9
Let Christ Rule in Your Heart

Remember the overall context as you study Paul's letter to the Colossians. Paul wants the congregation at Colossae to understand how dramatically their love for Christ should be changing their lives. Throughout this section, it is easy to get caught up in the minutia; however, you should be sure to see these things in the light of a life clothed with the blessings of Christ. Before we dive into the next section, take a moment to read through the entire letter to the Colossians.

Read Colossians 3:15-17

In this section of Scripture, Paul provides three compelling summary statements. He has just spent much time examining some specific things for the Colossians to remove from their lives and the things with which they should clothe themselves. He now gives them some more general guidelines to encompass everything they might encounter.

> What command is given in Colossians 3:15?

Think of what it means to rule. If you are the ruler of a kingdom, you will be responsible for the actions of your people and make critical decisions for your nation. Now, put this in the context of what Paul is saying here. The peace of Christ should guide our decision-making process. Every choice we make should be based on our reverence for Him.

I heard an interesting quote this week, and I am not sure exactly where it originated, but it ties in perfectly here: "When you became a Christian, all of the decisions for the rest of your life were made." If we allow Christ to rule our lives, our path has been laid before us. This does not mean it will be easy to follow––we are guaranteed it will not be (John 15:18-19); but if we hand our reins over to Christ, we are assured a victorious outcome.

> Do we allow the peace of Christ to rule in our lives, or do we make our daily decisions without thought or consideration of His reign in our lives?

How can we allow Christ to rule our decision-making process this week?

What command is given in Colossians 3:16?

Paul wants to ensure our minds are constantly centered on God's Word. Scripture does us no good if it stays on the pages of our favorite Bible or is painted as pretty artwork on our walls. It should richly dwell in our hearts and affect our actions on an extremely practical level.

We are instructed to let the Word of Christ dwell in us through song. Even before the giving of the Law, God's people practiced learning Scripture through song (Deuteronomy 31:22); music has the unique ability to make things stick in our hearts. This passage describes three types of songs that accomplish this: teaching, admonishing (correcting a wrong), and singing with thankfulness.

Describe how these types of songs can accomplish Paul's stated purpose.

What are some practical ways to incorporate singing into your daily routine so that you are participating in this act of dwelling on the Word of Christ through song?

Take a moment and read Deuteronomy 6:4-9. In what ways are these passages similar?

God has always desired His people to live permeated by His Word. If we don't study and dwell on God's Word daily, we will have trouble allowing Christ to be our ruler.

> What is the command given in Colossians 3:17?

Again, Paul emphasizes the importance of Jesus being the center of our lives. Whatever we do or say is to be done in honor of, in submission to, and with respect for Jesus and His authority. Every action should be governed by what we think Jesus would want us to do.

> Do you struggle with allowing your everyday decisions to be ruled by Christ? What are some specific areas that you steal control out of Jesus' hands? How can you work to let the choices you make this week be ruled by Christ?

Notice Paul's emphasis on thankfulness; he mentions this idea in these three verses. To the world, subjecting ourselves to someone else's authority seems terrible; however, in a spiritual context, it is incredibly freeing. We are guaranteed the ultimate happy ending if we submit to His authority. This should lead to an attitude of gratitude and joy.

> Do you struggle with an attitude problem? Can others see your thankful and humble spirit daily? What can you do to improve on these things?

Read Colossians 3:18-25

Remember, this is still in the context of Christ being the supreme ruler of our hearts. Paul gives us examples of actions and attitudes; now, we will see what those look like when applied in real-life situations. Again, looking at these actions through a worldly lens indicates weakness. In reality, looking through Christ's eyes and behaving humbly shows the utmost spiritual maturity.

> List the commands given in this section to each of these groups of people:
>
> - Wives:
>
>
> - Husbands:

Chapter 9 Let Christ Rule in Your Heart 85

- Children:

- Fathers:

- Slaves:

Describe Jesus' attitude according to Philippians 2:3-8.

In what ways are the attitudes displayed in these examples like the ultimate example of Christ?

This is what it looks like for Christ to rule their relationships. Each of these examples shows an absence of a self-serving attitude. They all follow Christ's example of emptying Himself for the good of others.

> What can you do this week to display the humble and submissive attitude of service that Christ displayed?

> According to Colossians 3:23-24, why are they behaving so peculiarly?

They are servants of the Lord, and He will reward them. We can easily get caught up in an attitude of entitlement. We deserve to be treated better, and we want justice. In reality, do we really deserve better? If Christ deeply humbled Himself, why should I think I am above doing the same? The truth behind the situation is this: If justice were dealt, we would not like the outcome!

Christians can rejoice that we have been granted an amazing inheritance in Heaven because of Christ's humility. We should not get so wrapped up in justice and fairness here on earth; God will dispatch consequences to those who have not submitted themselves to His will.

As you go about your daily walk this week, focus on Christ. Spend time every day in His Word. Allow Christ to sit in the driver's seat of your life; let Him make your daily decisions. "Whatever you do in word or deed, do all in the name of the Lord Jesus, giving thanks through Him to God the Father" (Colossians 3:17).

Chapter 10
Our Godly Influence

In chapter 4, Paul concludes his letter to the church at Colossae. He has a few critical thoughts to remind them of and several people he wants to relay messages to and from. This week, we will focus on his closing admonitions to the Colossians, and next week, we will look at the people he addresses. As always, begin your study by reading through this letter.

> **Read Colossians 4:1**

As you read through books and letters in your Bible, remember that the chapter divisions were not originally there. These were added later by men so that it would be easier to reference specific sections of Scripture. The first verse in Colossians 4 continues Paul's thoughts from the previous section on humility in our earthly relationships.

> What two things are masters to grant to their slaves according to Colossians 4:1?

Justice (*dikaios*) means following high standards of righteousness and fairness. *Fairness* (*isotes*) is the state of affairs being held in proper balance. These masters were to treat their slaves as equals and fellow human beings. Tuck this verse away in your brain; we will return to it in our examination of Philemon.

This may seem like an elementary principle; most of us can recite Matthew 7:12 by heart: "In everything, therefore, treat people the same way you want them to treat you, for this is the Law and the Prophets." We have been taught this "golden rule" since we were toddlers, yet we don't always apply it.

We must treat everyone respectfully, even if society tells us they rank below us. This includes people who work for us, people who aren't as smart as we think we are, and people with whom we disagree. It is very easy to get irritated at people whom we view as lesser in some way. We must remember that they are souls, too, and God loves them just as much as He loves us!

Chapter 10 Our Godly Influence

In what ways do you struggle with treating others with love and respect?

How can you improve on this today?

Read Colossians 4:2-4

In Colossians 3, Paul emphasizes different traits that Christians are to strip themselves of and then new qualities to put on in their place. He then shows us examples of what this attitude change would look like in our day-to-day relationships. Now, Paul is giving us specific actions we should engage in.

What command does Paul give in Colossians 4:2?

Paul places a heavy emphasis on prayer in all of his letters. *Devote* (*proskartereite*) means to attach oneself to or persist in something.

We should be so attached to our daily prayers that we never forget them. That isn't everything, though; attitude is also essential.

> According to this same verse (Colossians 4:2), describe the prayers we should have.

We should be "keeping alert" or staying awake in our prayers. We also see a thankful attitude once again playing an important part. In our daily prayer life, not only should we be consistent, but we should be aware of every word coming out of our mouths. We must constantly focus on what we are praying for and always direct our prayers with gratitude.

> Do you need more consistency in your prayer life or practice keeping your prayers earnest and heartfelt? How can you improve and make your prayers more persistent and thoughtful?

Chapter 10 Our Godly Influence

> What specific prayer requests does Paul make of them in Colossians 4:3-4?

Notice that every time Paul prays for someone or asks for prayers, his mind is focused on spiritual well-being rather than physical well-being. Remember, Paul is in prison while writing this letter, yet he doesn't ask them to deliver him from this punishment. He focuses on what is essential to the kingdom of God. He wants them to pray for open doors for him to preach the Word and for the right words to say when the opportunities present themselves.

When you say your daily prayers, do you ask for doors to open so that you can tell someone about God? Do you pray that when the doors are open, you will have the courage and the words to take full advantage of the situation? Be sure to add this to your prayer list!

> What spiritually-minded and evangelistic requests can you incorporate into your daily prayer life?

> **Read Colossians 4:5-6**
>
> According to Colossians 4:5, how should we behave toward "outsiders"?

When Paul talks about outsiders here, he is referring to those who are outside the body of Christ—non-Christians. Again, remember that these are also souls that God loves dearly. We must be sure we don't say something that would sour their opinion of Christianity. We represent Christ on earth, and we should reflect Him to others.

While it is natural to view this verse in the light of evangelism, the context of Colossians indicates another way to apply this passage. The problem the church in Colossae is having is that the outside world is shaking their faith in Christ. Their pagan and Jewish friends are causing them to doubt the sufficiency of Christ and thereby endangering their salvation. They don't need to walk with wisdom solely because they influence others, but they need to be wise about how others influence their faith.

> Are you "walking with wisdom" when it comes to non-Christians? In what ways can you work on being more evangelistically minded while not allowing them to influence you in ungodly ways?

How does Paul describe our speech in Colossians 4:6?

Grace (*chariti*) means attractiveness that invites a favorable reaction. There will always be those who reject God's message; however, let us act in a way that it is not our actions and attitude that they are rejecting. It is easy to allow ourselves to become condescending or snarky when dealing with some people. Remember, how we interact speaks volumes to others about the one we serve. Let us always ensure we never give people a reason to reject Christ on our account.

Are your words and actions attracting people to Christ or repelling them? How can you do a better job of making sure your speech toward non-Christians is always gracious and kind?

This week, as you interact with people, make sure you treat everyone with kindness and respect so that you do not hinder their path toward God. Spend some time focused on improving your prayer life, specifically in the area of evangelism. Ask God to open doors for you and give you the wisdom to make the most of each opportunity.

Notes

Chapter 11
Closing Thoughts

This week, we will review Paul's closing statements to the church in Colossae. Next week, we will begin our study of Paul's letter to Philemon. So, for the final time in our study together, spend some time reading through Colossians in one sitting.

Read Colossians 4:7-9

What two men does Paul send to them with news on his circumstances?

How is Tychicus described in Colossians 4:7 and Ephesians 6:21?

> How is Onesimus described in Colossians 4:9?

Paul had a very high opinion of Tychicus. He occasionally travels with Paul and is with him during his first and second imprisonments (Ephesians 6:21; 2 Timothy 4:12; Titus 3:12). Tychicus' companion on this trip is Onesimus. It is very likely that Onesimus is carrying an additional letter on this trip, the one we will be studying next week—Paul's letter to Philemon. We will discuss Onesimus in great detail at that time. The critical thing to note here is Paul's emphasis that Onesimus is a "faithful and beloved brother" and "one of [their] own people." This sets the stage for Paul's interaction with Philemon in his letter.

Read Colossians 4:10-14

Notice throughout Paul's letters the importance he places on personal relationships. He doesn't simply tell them to "be knit together" with love (Colossians 2:2); he shows them what that looks like through his relationships.

> List each person Paul sends greetings from and what is said about them.
> 1. _____ : _____

2. _____ : _____

3. _____ : _____

4. _____ : _____

5. _____ : _____

6. _____ : _____

Paul spends more time talking of Epaphras than the others, most likely because he is "one of their number." He is from their congregation, and Paul knows they want to hear how their hometown boy is doing. Paul thinks highly of this man because he only uses the phrase "bondslave of Jesus Christ" to describe a few other people: himself, Timothy, and Epaphras.

What specific things does Epaphras pray for on their behalf?

> Do you keep your brothers and sisters in Christ in your prayers? Do you pray for them to continue to stand firm in their faith? What are some ways you can implement this into your prayer life?

Interestingly, this is the only place in the New Testament where one congregation is told to greet the other. This is evidence that these groups must have been in close fellowship.

Paul ends this letter by reminding them to pass it along and ensure others read it. He also wants them to remember him while he is in prison.

Now that you have concluded your study of Paul's letter to the Colossian church, let's review it.

> Describe each chapter and what general ideas are found in them:
>
> Chapter 1:
>
>
> Chapter 2:

Chapter 11 Closing Thoughts

Chapter 3:

Chapter 4:

Choose one verse that you feel reflects the theme of Colossians and write it here:

Describe Christ according to Paul's words in this letter.

According to this letter, what does a faithful Christian look and act like?

What are three interesting facts you learned in this study that you didn't know before?

1.

2.

3.

List three ways you will challenge yourself to improve your spiritual life due to your study of Colossians.

1.

2.

3.

Chapter 12
Introduction to Philemon

This week, we begin our study of the fantastic little book of Philemon. This letter sets some high standards for equality in Christ that will resonate throughout the ages. While we don't struggle specifically with the issue of slavery in our modern American culture, there are many pertinent parallels to be made.

> **Before we begin, read Paul's letter to Philemon.**

This letter has three key players: Paul, Philemon, and Onesimus. We will examine each in detail, starting with Onesimus.

> What do we learn about Onesimus from Colossians 4:9?

"One of your number" means that he belongs to their congregation. From this verse, we can see that Onesimus is from Colossae; this would imply that Philemon is also.

> Read through Philemon again and list everything you discover about Onesimus.

Onesimus holds a special place in Paul's heart. Paul is the one who converted this runaway slave to Christianity. Onesimus is serving Paul in prison, but Paul sends him back to his master in Colossae.

> Read through this letter once more and list everything you find about Philemon.

Try not to jump to the conclusion that just because Philemon owns slaves, he is an evil man. While the ownership of slaves certainly defies the nature of a Christian relationship with a fellow human (something we will look into more in our next chapter), it was a part of the Roman culture and an issue Paul is wise enough to handle with care.

Chapter 12 Introduction to Philemon

Paul thinks highly of Philemon and says so many times throughout this letter. Not only is Philemon a wealthy man, but he is also using his wealth to further God's kingdom. The church meets in his home. Philemon has a deep, abiding love for his Christian brothers and sisters. This love is about to be challenged, and the foundations of his social structure would be shaken. Onesimus, his runaway slave, has gained equal footing with him as a Christian brother.

> Once again, read Paul's letter to Philemon and list anything you have discovered about Paul.

Onesimus and Tychicus are likely carrying both of these letters (Colossians and Philemon) to the church in Colossae when they come. Since they read the letters to the churches publicly, Philemon probably listened to the entire letter of Colossians upon its arrival.

> List some key points in the book of Colossians that would have prepared Philemon's heart to receive this difficult message.

> Read Colossians 4:1 and describe how this verse directly deals with the issues addressed in the book of Philemon.

Paul's extreme wisdom and guidance of the Holy Spirit are powerful in this letter. As we examine this writing, it is essential to understand the matter of Christian equality, and we should pay particular attention to how Paul approaches the situation. Dealing with others can often be a delicate matter, and Paul treats this encounter with the utmost care and respect. He is cautious to get his message across without offending Philemon. This letter is a fantastic example of boldly proclaiming the truth with extreme tact and respect.

> Read through Philemon one last time this week and write a simple outline of the text.
> - Philemon 1-3:
>
> - Philemon 4-7:
>
> - Philemon 8-16:
>
> - Philemon 17-20:
>
> - Philemon 21-22:
>
> - Philemon 23-25:

Chapter 12 Introduction to Philemon   105

Keywords:
- Christ (*Christos*)
- Jesus (*Iesous*)
- Brother (*adelphos*)
- Lord (*Kyrios*)
- Love (*agapao*)
- Rejoice (*chairo*)

What do we learn about each of these keywords from Philemon?

Jesus/Christ/Lord:

Love:

Brother:

Rejoice:

Using as many keywords as possible, write a sentence or two describing the theme of Philemon.

As you study this book, consider the reflective nature of these relationships. Paul appeals to Philemon on behalf of Onesimus. Onesimus's relationship with Paul is the same as our relationship with Christ. He is there to appeal for us. We will look more deeply into this parallel in our next chapter; however, keep it in mind as you read this letter throughout the week.

Notes

Chapter 13
Love on Display

Our study through the text of Philemon will only be one lesson long. Even though this letter is concise, it holds some beautiful applications for our everyday lives. Because it is only one chapter, I encourage you to read through it each day this week. This will help you keep your study in context and increase your understanding of this fantastic little letter.

Read Philemon 1-7

> How does Paul describe himself in Philemon 1?

Because of this description, most scholars incorporate Philemon into the list of "prison epistles," including Ephesians, Philippians, and Colossians.

> How does Paul describe Philemon in this letter?

> Verse 2 states that Philemon hosts the church in his house. What does this imply about Philemon?

Philemon must have been wealthy to have a home big enough to host the church gathering. This assumption is also confirmed by the fact that he has slaves. An important thing to note is that Philemon uses his wealth to serve the kingdom of God. He does not have to have the church in his home; this speaks highly of his character right from the outset of the letter.

> Who else besides Philemon is included as the recipient of this letter?

Notice that while the main subject of this letter is Philemon, Apphia, and Archippus are also addressed. They are likely either

Philemon's wife and son or his brother and sister. Since this iss a personal letter, Paul likely wishes to address all of the members of Philemon's household.

> What specific things does Paul include in his prayers about Philemon?

We've discussed this concept in previous lessons, so we won't dwell here long. Again, we see Paul praying for others in a very spiritual way. Not only does he ask God to bless Philemon in his work, but he thanks God for his love and faith. I challenge you to take the rest of this month and choose one new person a day. Thank God for this person in specific ways and ask God to help her with whatever spiritual goals she is trying to accomplish.

> Why would Paul say he takes comfort in Philemon's love?

I believe that Paul is taking comfort in Philemon's love for his brothers and sisters in Christ because love is the crux of the message he is about to share. He is about to challenge Philemon's concept of who a brother is. He is reassured by the fact that Philemon takes this seriously and knows that Philemon will heed his plea.

> If Paul addressed you personally, would he take comfort in your love? Why or why not?

> What steps can you take this week to refresh the hearts of your fellow Christians through your actions?

Would he know that your love for God and others is so important that you would be willing to humble yourself in any way necessary to adhere to God's will? Let us always strive to have the attitude and love of Philemon.

Read Philemon 8-16

> What is the purpose of Paul's letter to Philemon?

Chapter 13 Love on Display

Philemon's slave Onesimus had run away and, during this journey, has become a Christian. Paul refers to Onesimus as "my child," implying that he is the one who brought him to Christ. I want to dwell on this for a moment. Do you remember where Paul is when he wrote Colossians and Philemon? He is in prison! Paul never lets his circumstances dictate his devotion to God, which is evident here. His top priority is constantly to win souls for Christ.

> In what ways do you let your circumstances dictate your level of service to God? What can you do this week that will help you have a more steadfast relationship of service to our Lord and help keep His will as your top priority?

Notice the approach Paul takes when talking to Philemon. Even though he has the authority as an apostle to command him to accept Onesimus as a brother, he doesn't want Philemon to be compelled by force. He appeals to Philemon out of love on behalf of Onesimus. Paul admonishes and teaches his fellow Christians in many different ways; he often uses powerful language and harsh words. This is not the method he takes with Philemon.

> Think back to Colossians 4:6. What command does Paul give in this verse?

In context, we can see that this verse specifically refers to our behavior towards those who are not Christians, but the concept also applies to our brothers and sisters in Christ. Paul shows great wisdom and approaches his audiences as he feels would be most effective for them. He may have known a stern command would have hardened Philemon's heart, so instead, he appealed to his loving nature.

This is something valuable to remember as we approach others for various reasons. We should not only consider how we want to deal with the situation; we must think about the approach that would be most effective with this person. Some people do best with a blunt, to-the-point message, while others may respond better to a humbler method. Remember, when approaching a brother or sister about an issue, the most important thing is not to prove you are right but to see that God's will is being done.

> Have you ever witnessed a situation softened because of the wise way a brother or sister in Christ approached it?

Chapter 13 Love on Display 113

> What are some practical ways you can better approach confrontation in a way that caters to the sensitivities of your brothers and sisters in Christ?

> What does Paul say in verse 11 about Onesimus?

Paul uses a play on words in this verse. Onesimus's name means "useful." Paul claims that once he was useless, he now lives up to his name and is useful to both Paul and Philemon. Clearly, Onesimus is very special to Paul, and he wants to communicate that to Philemon by calling him "my very heart." What he is asking won't be easy, so he wants to make sure Philemon understands how personal this request is.

> What challenges do you think Philemon would have faced accepting Onesimus as a brother in Christ?

This would have been a challenging request for Philemon to adhere to. Even if he is willing to love Onesimus as Paul did right away, he will face much ridicule in society for doing so. Also, consider if Philemon is genuinely devoted to doing God's will and treating Onesimus as a spiritual equal; one could conclude that the repercussions would eventually lead to Onesimus' release.

Paul asked Philemon to become a social outcast for Christ's sake and his new brother's love. God expects the same of us. We should always be willing to put the will of God ahead of our social standing. Have you ever hesitated to share the Gospel with someone because of what he or she might think of you? Have you neglected to address a spiritually damaging issue with your sister in Christ because you aren't sure she will take it well? Are you hesitant to publicly talk about your beliefs because they aren't politically correct? Which is more important: to do God's will or be deemed socially acceptable and liked by everyone?

> In what ways have you compromised your spirituality for the sake of social acceptance?

Chapter 13 Love on Display

What can you do this week to be bolder in your faith?

Read Philemon 17-23

What does Paul ask of Philemon in verse 17?

What does Paul offer Philemon in verses 18 and 19?

Paul wants to be sure that upon Onesimus' return, there are no issues that will cause problems later on. He takes personal responsibility for Onesimus' previous actions and offers to repay any amount owed. This might be because Onesimus stole something when he left, or it may simply be the financial burden of a runaway slave. Paul is a living example of the fact that the Gospel of Christ can completely change the shape of someone's life. People can change, and Paul knows that Onesimus needs to be given the same grace that Paul was when he turned his life around.

> Do we struggle with believing the Gospel of Christ can truly reform the worst of sinners? How does this idea impact our evangelistic efforts?

> Think of one person you have written off as "unchangeable." What can you do to reach him with Christ's love this week?

> How does Paul and Onesimus's relationship closely mirror our relationship with Christ?

In the last few verses, Paul follows up his urging by expressing confidence in the fact that Philemon would do the right thing. Once again, he shows his wisdom in dealing with others. When someone expects you to do well, you at least try to live up to that expectation. Paul wants to give Philemon every reason to succeed in how he accepts Onesimus.

This account can serve as a beautiful example of what Christ has done. When we become Christians, He takes full responsibility. He is the mediator between God and us, just as Paul is between Philemon and Onesimus. Any amount previously owed Christ paid for us on the cross. We could not have a better advocate.

> How does this picture of Christ in the book of Philemon follow the image of Christ we see in Colossians?

Studying these two beautiful letters holds so much practical application in our daily walk. From how we treat our brothers and sisters in Christ to the conviction to stand firm in the midst of temptation, Paul gives us so much meat to chew on. We also get a front-row seat to the supremacy and sufficiency of Christ and the importance of being in a relationship with Him. As we conclude this study, I challenge you not to allow this to be empty knowledge gained. Put these things into practice in the service to God and His kingdom.

Works Cited

Arndt, William, Frederick W. Danker and Walter Bauer. *A Greek-English Lexicon of the New Testament and Early Christian Literature,* 3rd ed. Chicago, IL: Logos Bible Software. 2000.

Martin, Ernest D. Believers *Church Bible Commentary: Colossians, Philemon.* Scottdale, PA: Herald Press, 1993.

Olbricht, Owen D. and Bruce McLarty. *Truth for Today Commentary: Colossians and Philemon.* Searcy, AR: Resource Publications, 2005.

www.ingramcontent.com/pod-product-compliance
Lightning Source LLC
Chambersburg PA
CBHW061809070526
44586CB00024B/2775